T0123264

When the Sun Dimmed

Leela Maharaj

authorHOUSE®

AuthorHouse™
1663 Liberty Drive
Bloomington, IN 47403
www.authorhouse.com
Phone: 1 (800) 839-8640

Published by AuthorHouse   07/11/2015

ISBN: 978-1-5049-2218-0 (sc)
ISBN: 978-1-5049-2219-7 (e)

Library of Congress Control Number: 2015911012

Print information available on the last page.

Contents

To my husband and children

PRELIMINARY DEFINITION

What Is a Chemical Imbalance?

Chemical imbalance is one buzzword used today to explain mental health problems. Chemical imbalances can exist in the neural pathway system of the brain and lead to emotional pain. Understanding how this works is important to progress and recovery.

Social anxiety is often associated with precipitating events, situations, and circumstances in a person's environment. Social anxiety develops over time. The brain learns how to be socially anxious, a process known as cognitive structuring. In this process, the brain learns how and what to fear. If you're afraid of a certain event, this event might be the triggers to create anxiety. The neurons in your brain create confusion.

No one is born with social anxiety. There is no gene that codes for social anxiety, and there is no immutable set of genes causing social anxiety to occur. Social anxiety has more to do with the environment than with genetics.

Even if a trait is genetically influenced, that does not mean it will cause illness in any given individual. Social anxiety may not occur unless events, situations, and circumstances combine to encourage its development.

The feeling of anxiety is a rush of adrenaline and cortisol, two hormones in the body. Cognitive (learning) therapy is a method of treating social anxiety. As you learn ways to manage anxiety through cognitive therapy and then practice them, the cognitive method creates a new neural pathway. The more you practice, the more this new neural pathway grows. Progress may be slow at first, just as when you learn any new skill, but if you continue to practice, you will continue to get better. Through practice, this habit becomes more and more automatic. Reprogramming the brain to create new habits changes the neural pathways in the brain. How do brain chemicals, neurochemistry, and "imbalances" of brain chemistry fit here?

Your neural pathways and associations influence the neurochemicals that pass through the synapses. Your neurochemistry is determined by your neural pathways and associations.

Medication can change your brain chemistry temporarily. But medications have no power to change neural pathways. There is relief, but no cure, for social anxiety in medication. There is a temporary chemical change in your brain from medication, but it lasts only as long as the medication lasts. A permanent solution involves changing the brain.

The only permanent solution to neurochemical imbalances is change within the neural pathways and associations. This can only be done by learning new strategies. These new strategies must be practiced. Repetition is the key to this cure. Without repetition, neural pathways and associations cannot change. This change is the permanent solution for social anxiety.

CHAPTER 1

Chemical Imbalance

This is my experience and my story, which I would like to share with you. I hope to save you from experiences as painful as mine. I was forty-nine years old and had undergone a hysterectomy, which set off a chain reaction of horrific experiences. Later I learned from my doctor that I was suffering from a chemical imbalance due to the changes in my body. Today, after many months of struggle, I understand that my situation is not unique; I have learned that both genders can experience these same symptoms for many different reasons.

Many changes can occur in both men and women and cause depression or anxiety, though this occurs in women more often. But depression and anxiety are not purely female issues. I encourage you to educate yourself about these conditions.

Depression and anxiety are topics that make people anxious, so we may be uncomfortable speaking about them. This is why we may feel ashamed, insecure, and unequipped to deal with these problems. I say to you now, that the cure for any problem is knowledge.

What causes depression? We do not really know the reason for depression, but we know that chemicals called neurotransmitters (specifically serotonin, norepinephrine, and dopamine) regulate mood, cognition, sleep, appetite, and behavior. When these neurotransmitters are out of balance, they create imbalance in the brain.

Depression can have a considerable effect on us. The more we know about depression, the more patient, compassionate, and understanding we will become. Your depressed loved one will need time to recover. Communication is the key. Depression can be treated with the help of medication, family support, and therapeutic instruction. Depression can be cured. To make these changes permanent takes consistency, persistence, and repetition.

Women are the strength in a home, and men are the support. A woman plays the roles of a mother, sister, friend, and nurse, and sometime she provides financial support for her household. Men, on the other hand, traditionally bear the responsibility of being the main financial support in the home and are the authority figures at home.

A woman may add tasks to her already-packed schedule, which she manages in the time she has available. Both men and women ignore self-care to take care of children and the home. This book is intended to alert both men and women to the changes that take place within and how stress can become destructive. Pay attention to what is happening to your body and your mind to avoid reaching the breaking point. We all need accurate information on preventing this burnout.

Natural changes in the female body can cause women to suffer from chemical imbalances that cause anxiety and depression. Women, you need to educate yourselves on menopause, chemical imbalances, and anxiety and depression. First teach yourselves, and then share this information with others.

Men or husband be supportive to your partner. Their knowledge may be helpful to you. Understand the women in your life, for in any relationship understanding is necessary. To lose a partner may break you mentally and physically.

Daughters, learn to understand your mothers. As young women, you experience anxiety and depression. Her advice and information may be the key to avoid unnecessary suffering.

Sons, learn to understand your mothers, they are your first teachers. Learn from their experiences, and become compassionate, caring gentlemen. The world will soon be under your control.

Let us teach others from our experiences, help each other, and show them the path to happiness. Share your knowledge and lift the ones who have fallen by giving them the courage to hope. Let us increase their faith, give them strength, shower them with love, and bring happiness into their lives again. Love them and make them understand that they are valuable and they will overcome this obstacle with the correct medication and with your support.

Women, support each other, for you are your best supporters. Don't forget that you are your sisters' protectors, not their worst enemies.

Men, do not be ashamed when faced with these difficulties or discomforts. Know that there is help and that you can seek that help.

Chapter 2

Why Does Depression Occur?

There is no way to know when, why, or how depression begins. There is no way to tell exactly when a person will fall victim to this condition, but learning and reading about these topics will provide an education that may save you. Get information on menopause, chemical imbalances, and how they are related to anxiety and depression. Read about these topics, talk to your doctors, and insist that they educate you. You can also talk to your mother, your father, or a friend who might have experienced these mood issues. Ask what medications are available to you. It is never too early to learn. Changes can begin as early as your teens. Eventually, when we think we have everything under control, we are greeted by this big surprise—something is happening to us, something is wrong, and our first reaction is panic.

Is any type of person at special risk? No. Whether housewife or professional, depression does not discriminate. It can afflict anyone at any time.

Why does it happen?

There is really no single reason. Depression does not happen because of physical or emotional weakness. It may not be preventable, but knowledge can make us more prepared to deal with it if it does happen. Your doctors can prescribe medication to reduce the symptoms if it does. There is no reason to be ashamed of this illness.

Be open, be brave, and talk to your doctors, family members, and trustworthy friends. This is no shame or blot on your life. Be proud of who you are. Speak about yourself and ask questions. Going through changes only makes you more beautiful and stronger. Growing older is not a curse—it is a privilege. You are blessed by God, and as you grow older, you will get more help from God because you have built a relationship with Him.

When we were young, life was busy, full of excitement and fun, a hectic merry-go-round. Life is still fun as we grow older. With experience and God's support, life is good. Ladies, these changes do not make you less feminine. You do not become invisible or lose your beauty. In fact your beauty is enhanced with grace and elegance. Men, this is a frightening experience, but please don't shy away or hide from the world. As hard as this experience may be, you must face it, seek help, and educate yourselves to fight this disease.

When you are depressed, if you pay attention to people who make you feel incapable, you will see that they are still expecting from you. They still expect you to take care of the home and of the family, and you continue to do that. You are suffering from an imbalance, and that doesn't mean you have become incapable.

If your spouse doesn't want to understand this change, know that there is help and you can seek it. You are still the same, but sometimes your normal activities might become difficult to handle. However, you are not crazy.

As a woman, do what I did. I spoke to my husband, my sisters, my children, my mother, and my doctor. I was advised on the best way to proceed, the best medication, and how to adjust and understand what is happening to me. My husband, my children, and all my family members became my strength. They support me because I made the decision to talk and explain, and this is why I got a constructive response. This is the first step toward becoming strong and moving to wellness.

My dear friends don't feel alone. Many others have fallen victim to this illness. More will suffer from it over time, so learn and become teachers to others.

You are not crazy, so don't let anyone say that you are. Ignorant people lack compassion. It is my wish to teach, share, and help others who have found themselves in this situation, to educate those who might get here, and to prevent others from suffering as badly as I did.

Friends, no longer must you hide yourselves away or remain silent. Speak up! You will learn something that will be helpful to you. Sharing and love will empower you to become happy.

Take time to listen to good counsel. We can learn valuable lessons through listening. Hiding in silence can destroy you. Fight and become victorious.

Remember to say this mantra every day.

> Today I will smile,
> because it makes me feel better.
> Today I will smile,
> because it is good for my health.
> Today I will smile,
> because a smile is what it takes to bring success, to share love,
> to fill me with energy, and to make me feel like flying.
>
> If only I knew the value of my smile,
> I would never have let it fade or allowed a single thought to push it out.
> Today I know the power of my smile, and today I will never let it fade.

CHAPTER 3

The Doom Day

Such exhaustion! I felt overtaken, as if something was draining my body and mind. I could not understand this tiredness. There was no reason for this to happen; I was not overworking. At that point I realized something was wrong.

My first reaction was withdrawal from my family and friends, as I tried to fix what was happening. This was like drowning. The more I remained silent and stayed in bed, the worse I felt. Eventually I began to fear that I was going crazy. At this point I broke down and began crying. My husband was very upset, seeing me crying so much. He begged me to talk to my children, who live abroad. I did not want them to see me crying; I felt that it made me looked weak. I kept these feelings bottled up until I felt unable to breathe. I wanted answers and miracles. I needed a quick fix. Where could I find this miracle? I begged God to help me. But nothing changed.

My choices were swim or drown, and I chose to swim. I called my sister, Lisa, and told her that something was wrong with me. I needed help, and she made time to come to me. I realized that my mind was turning against me like an enemy. How can someone's own mind turn against her? Is this possible? Yes. Today I understand what I always knew: I am a soul inside this body. This soul is the boss of my body, but because this soul had taken the back seat for so many years, my mind saw itself as the boss. But without my soul, this mind has no power and would not be alive.

So the big question is, "Why is my mind fighting me, instilling fear in me, and just disturbing me? It is trying to take control of my body? In doing this, it is removing my happiness, my smile, and my zeal for life. There are scientific terms for what was taking place in my body; the most popular words are *menopause* and *chemical imbalance*. These are real biological influences that affect women. They involve no bleeding, but they can cause internal destruction that requires medical attention. Ladies, set aside your pride! Don't listen to negative comments. This suffering entity is your mind, and you need to fix it. A sick mind can destroy a good, happy life. Don't allow this to destroy you. I have made the decision to fight and take back control. My happiness and laughter are my greatest treasures. I want my happiness back.

How do I take control?

I take control through understanding, by taking baby steps toward positive thinking. Most importantly, I stay positive and maintain my faith that all will be well.

That's more easily said than done.

Continue to remind yourself to stay positive. Don't blame yourself. Understand that this imbalance will be restored. The body will recalibrate its estrogen levels slowly but surely, and you will begin feeling your happiness returning. Do not underestimate the mind, it has the capability to repair and restore. You have to make choices, show courage, and have patience. Learn to share your thoughts and accept help. This is the first step toward recovery. Here is a positive thought that my daughter Virmala shared with me: "Be patient with YOU through this transition period."

CHAPTER 4

The Onset of Depression

As my sense of doom settled in, I observed these signs.

1. Withdrawal
2. Frequently feeling upset and hurt
3. Uncommunicative behavior
4. Increased muscle pain
5. Exhaustion
6. Anxiety
7. Fear of going crazy
8. Sadness without cause
9. Loss of appetite
10. Shame

The mood fueled by all these factors is the worst feeling one could experience, like a dark tunnel with no escape. I now realize how early those sensations began with me, but like everyone else, I was too busy to address my darkening mood. Did I pay attention? No. Did I ask for help? No.

I cannot really say that my experience was entirely a surprise. I saw all the signs, but I chose to look away. Today I am sorry I did not respond more hastily, but I have not given up. Depression comes on stealthily, like a thief; it steals your emotions, kills your happiness, and destroys your appetite. It makes you confused and fearful.

What do you do when this happens? Just as you know that death will come but can never prepare yourself for it; it is hard to be prepared for depression. Happy people are carefree and also, sometimes, careless.

My good friends, let's remember to take care of our total health. Let us understand this mind and not give it the power to ruin us. Treat it with respect, but remember that we don't have to accept the bad thoughts that pull us down, destroy our happiness, and drain our energy. Our minds can fluster us and lead us into anger. After that, there is no control. We stay upset and void our happiness, and then what happens? Life becomes tasteless, and it takes time before you can return to normal. Void of happiness, you cannot speak nicely, and that is precious time lost and gone forever.

This is why we must have good, clean thoughts to help us retain a high level of happiness. Feed your intellect the correct food for your mind to function well and not to fail you or work against you.

Stop negativity from taking up space in your head. Find a way to get rid of it. Instead, fill your head with joy, which gives us the energy to conquer.

I advise you to become carefree, not careless. Take care to fill the mind with the correct material and feed it the proper food. A happy mind can never fail you. We all need to understand what our thoughts can do. Learn from mistakes and do not allow ego to engulf you. This brings no benefit. Filling the mind with many good qualities will bring benefit to yourself and others.

Share love, show compassion, and practice training the mind to do well. In times of stress, these habits will serve us well.

A mind trained to think positively will maintain that habit, even when depression and anxiety test it. With this training and proper medication, you can recover. Never give up. Relief will come in time. Be patient and accept the help offered to you.

CHAPTER 5

Mental Tiredness

I felt well, like my normal self again. Smiling, laughing, and talking felt awesome. I was doing all that I was accustomed to doing. I advise you, when you have that awesome feeling that comes with recovery, to go slowly. Don't overwork. You may still tire and feel stress quickly. Overreaching is not optimal. Do a little work and get to bed early. Give your body time to adjust to the changes that are taking place. This gentle routine will help you to stay balanced.

Let me share one experience: the first time when I began to feel well again. I was so happy to feel better that I went right back being that busy person. I shifted into high gear and did not think twice about pacing myself. I was so happy to be happy that I forgot that I was, in fact, still recovering. I took no precautions to conserve my energy. By 2 PM I was totally tired, and the niggling fear began creeping back. My decision to work so hard had not been the right choice. The fear of not recovering returned as my energy level dropped, and my hope took a dip as well. Horrific thoughts returned. I understood that I had been getting stronger. I was just careless and did not conserve my energy. As soon as my negative-thinking mind got the opportunity to take control, it did. It created all these negative thoughts that pulled my whole spirit and body down. A person can begin to feel lifeless, living without hope, but I know that there is hope within me, even when the hope is hard to locate. I felt as if I had been hit by a tornado. I then tried to take support from those around me and from God. I do have a strong support system and loved ones to talk to me, and they make me laugh. These simple, little tools are big cures for this illness called depression.

Some important points

1. When you feel like your old self again, pace yourself. Enjoy your activities but remember that your overall well-being is more important than work.
2. Plan your work and do it in small steps.
3. Remember the lessons that you have learned each day and keep reminding yourself of these lessons, good quotes, or little jokes. These are stimuli to keep the mind strong. You will get better because, each day, you grow stronger.

4. The more you understand what is happening and learn what triggers your low moods, the better you will be equipped to handle your problems.

5. Remember that your loved ones are your biggest support. There is no shame in accepting their help. Never feel insecure. A sense of security is a protective shield. Do not lose your shield.

6. Trust your doctors and talk to them. Share your fears and concerns. Ask them how you can help yourself during this time. Build a good relationship with your doctor. Some doctors may be kind enough to share their mobile numbers with you in case you have an emergency and need to hear strong words of encouragement. This kind of contact with your doctor can reassure and comfort you during a crisis.

7. Never let shame keep you from asking for help.

8. Never forget to ask God for guidance and support.

9. Be willing to accept help. Without help, you may not find a solution.

Through many days of suffering, I continued to believe in a good outcome. One of my supporters was my sister Gayatri, who did not even live in the same country with me but continued to call me, email me, and send three or four cards per week. She found jokes and riddles and emailed them to me, for which I felt grateful and blessed. On one of my bad days, she shared this joke with me.

There were three retirees, each with a hearing loss. They were taking a walk one fine March day. One remarked to the other, "Windy, isn't it?"

"No," the second man replied, "It's Thursday."

And the third man chimed in, "So am I, so let's have a Coke."

I bless the many people who share with me, love me, and help me.

Chapter 6

The Impact of Depressive Fatigue

Depression begins with tiredness, which I now understand is not just ordinary fatigue. It is mental tiredness that drains your energy and leaves you feeling lifeless. This is when the mind takes control with negative thoughts and confuses the body. Then you get anxious, and understanding seems a thing of the past. Without understanding, reasoning cannot take place, so no solutions are forthcoming. This is the worst form of fatigue. Physical tiredness lets you rest and recover, but mental tiredness is continually draining.

How do you conquer mental tiredness?

My daughter Virmala, who saw me suffering this energy drain, shared a technique with me.

"Mommy," she said, "breathe in slowly and exhale slowly. Quiet all the thoughts in your head. Now think of a safe place, somewhere you can go and feel safe." I closed my eyes and began to think of a safe place. Virmala continued to guide me. "Relax your eyes, breathe slowly, allow your thoughts to quiet, and allow your body to relax."

I recommend that people suffering from depression practice this method. It helps to keep you smiling. Depression gives us a very serious expression, and a smile produces energy. By making an effort to smile, you can raise your endorphin level. Increased endorphin levels help you to become happy. Happiness means production of energy.

This is one way to take back control of your mind. Another way is asking for help. Talking about what is happening, telling others your thoughts and fears, may help. Do not try to stay busy with work during a depressive episode. Rather, take time to fix what has gone wrong and recover. Understand that yours is a serious problem and that it is important to fix it now. Letting it wait until later may be harmful.

Increase your exercise, If you do not attend a gym, try walking for twenty to thirty minutes. Exercise helps and is another way to lift that heavy weight that tries to take over your body.

Don't expect a miracle, though I couldn't help wanting one. There are no miracles. I tried many methods and realized that success came from positive thoughts. Positive thinking is the key to your success. A positive attitude is one key to recovery but not, in itself, a cure. Great effort is needed to become well, plus determination and much faith. We need human support and love, as well as comforting words. You need to visit your doctor and to see a specialist who can treat clinical depression.

Depression causes loss of appetite. Even so, nutritious food is vital. To regain control, you must nourish your brain and body. A weak body and mind open the way to destruction.

Remember that you are the star writer, producer, and director of the production known as yourself. Commit today to a positive attitude, which is the first step to healing. Keep up your hope with the conviction that there is relief and you will be healed.

Think of your illness as a rough wave that you will learn to ride. It may throw you down, but you will learn from each wave. Hope confers strength and courage. Be honest with yourself: Hope is not a miracle, but it helps us to become positive.

Your prospects may look dim, but remember that this pessimism will pass, and remember also that situations are rarely as bad as they may seem.

Smile and turn up the volume of the radio, clap to the tune, and tap your feet. Guess what? A smile will come.

CHAPTER 7

Seek Your Doctor's Advice

Depression is a somatic illness as well as a mental one; do not think you can cure yourself. You need medical help. With your doctor's support and guidance, you will get better. This is no easy situation. Facing it alone is like fighting the waves from the ocean without proper gears.

Don't become disheartened when the doctor gives you the facts and history of this illness. The truth can be painful, but we need to know the truth. Only then can we choose our tactics. I have firsthand experience listening to this information. I asked myself if it really was useful to know all these facts about my diagnosis. Now I believe that this knowledge is useful. Information like this should be given gently and in small doses. Only when you listen and understand can you find solutions to make this transition easier.

Do not be afraid to learn about and discuss your diagnosis. This learning process is the only way to find solutions. Work through your fear and keep faith. Faith gives you the strength to overcome. Do not lose hope, though you might feel discouraged, as if your world is ending. This feeling will pass. Happiness will return.

Follow your doctor's advice, take your medications, and continue speaking to him. Make him aware of your worries and concerns. His advice should help you to regain some of your strength and control. I find that talking openly about what is disturbing me at any given moment brings relief. When no one was around for me to talk with, I began writing my thoughts down, which also helped me.

Each day presents new feelings and experiences. Some may be good, and others may be awful. Just do the best you can. Do not stay inside the house and feel uncomfortable. Instead, go outside, meet people, and talk with them. You might want to think of volunteering your services, for helping others is helping yourself. Make an effort to smile, stay positive, and remind yourself that depression will remit and happiness will flow back in. Trust your doctor, your loved ones, your friends, and, most importantly, trust yourself.

My daughter, who is like an angel, helped me during my many bad episodes. She has been amazing. God bless you, Virmala, for helping me, sharing with me, and always being ready to dance with me. My husband supported me even though some time he did not understand what was happening. Shivani and Jay, even though so far away continued to share so much love and care and made time to share kind words and smiles with me. Thank you.

Never give up. I never gave up. Know that there are many people out there who love and care for you.

As I mentioned before, hope gives us strength. Words are powerful tools; we must use them carefully and learn to communicate clearly. We must not underestimate how powerful our words and thoughts are—not only to the person we address, but also to ourselves. Words can do great good or great harm. Your words or a shared smile can help you and the other person. Be careful and use them wisely. Understand the power of the words "I will" and "I can."

Stay out of yesterday, wait for tomorrow, and live in the present. Then the past cannot destroy the present. Just do your best today, for today is the important day. Be honest with yourself. Only then can reality be your guide. Remember that by talking and listening, you can learn much.

When choosing your doctor, check. Research their backgrounds. Talk to other people to identify the most suitable doctor. Your doctor is crucial to your improvement, so you want the best doctor. Some doctors care for their patients, and some doctors care for their patients' money. This is why you must check credentials and patient reviews before you choose your doctor.

CHAPTER 8

God, the Doctor
of All Doctors

You now have a better understanding of what an imbalance is and what it can do to you. You are already experiencing and facing the many difficulties from this illness. You have learned that when suffering from this illness, to keep it a secret or to try to hide the symptoms may only make matters worse and your recovery time longer. The right thing to do is tell someone, ask for help, and see your doctor.

You now know the importance of medication, and you must visit a doctor. Don't hide away or let anyone influence you into not using your medication by telling you all the side effects. Most tablets have side effects, but they also do a good job in helping you to recover. Your doctor is a qualified person and specializes in persons suffering from this illness.

Never give up hope for improvement and recovery. You possess strength and courage. Religion can bolster that strength and courage.

All human beings have one heavenly Father. He is the Doctor of all doctors. A medical doctor may say there is no hope for a patient, but God would never give up hope on you. A patient with faith and trust in God has an advantage in recovery. It is no miracle, but they draw their strength from their faith in God, and this facilitates their recovery.

God is your first Father. He is the Father of the soul that resides in your body. You have a Heavenly Father and an earthly father. God is all-merciful. When you need Him, you can call out to Him, and He comes and carries you and helps ease your trouble. I don't want you to think that God will come running in whatever situation or trouble you encounter. You must talk to God, tell Him your troubles, have faith, and trust Him to make the right decision. Faith in God gives us the strength to hope. Hope facilitates recovery.

Those who lose hope stop trying. One can never succeed without trying. When there is no one to turn to, try turning to God. He is merciful. We are the ones who lack mercy for one another. Humans may turn away and refuse to help or to forgive one another. God, however, loves all of us. He would never cause us sorrow. If God were not merciful, we would not address Him as the Merciful One.

If you have true love for God, you must trust Him, and then rest assured that He will hear your call.

I emphasize that, before becoming ill, I had a relationship with God. I habitually say good morning to God in the morning and good night to Him at night. I understood who God is. My relationship with God is like a bond between father and child. If I do not love and respect God, I cannot receive His good regard. Therefore, when I became ill, I turned to God first. I asked many questions, I cried, and I asked God to help me. With God's help, I got all my family's support; my doctors could not have been more caring, and those to whom I turned were willing to help me. This is the miracle of God's help. Don't sit and think that God is sitting on a throne and would descend to touch your head. God will send the help you require. Be patient, respectful, and loving.

Life is what you make it. You are responsible for your own outcome. This sounds complicated, but this is the reality of this world's drama. We all have a part to play and must play it well. Your decision creates your future. Truth may sound hurtful, but it is the truth that lifts you and makes your future brighter.

God gives us what we need, not what we want. For human beings, wants are never-ending. All God requires from us is an honest heart and love.

In my experience, when I asked for help, God sent help in many different ways. I felt relief; I felt that strength growing within me. Continuous love surrounded me. God cannot come to us Himself, but He can send angels. My angels were my caring doctors, Dr. Sirju, Dr. Lalla, Dr. Balliram, and Dr. Ramtahal.

God is the highest power. Let no one shake your faith in God. I continue to feel God's healing hands on me. My faith is very strong, and now no one can convince me that it is impossible to recover fully from this illness, because I know what God's touch can do. It heals. I understand that, with every trial and tribulation we face, we grow stronger and better. You will learn many lessons from these problems; try looking at them differently instead of blaming others and looking for answers in all the wrong places. I know that every problem has a solution. And we must use the experience we gain to help another human being. First we learn from our experiences, and then we can guide others.

God, I put my trust in You, and all I ask is that You allow me to love You.

CHAPTER 9

Wisdom from My Daughter

These words were shared by my daughter, with much love, and they filled me with encouragement. I want to share her message with my readers.

Virmala, my daughter, I want to thank you for caring and sharing with me. My blessings will always be with you.

To Mommy,

One of the strongest women God has blessed me to know. Today I want you to remember to truly enjoy life every moment. Sometimes it's good to slow down and smell the roses. When thoughts queue up in your mind, the never-ending lists of things to do, please reconsider the urgency of these tasks.

What is the urgency of getting all these tasks done?

Remember to take deep breaths, inhale, hold for two seconds, and exhale. As you exhale, feel the thoughts and ideas, or "traffic jam," as you call it, disappearing. How do we dissolve this so-called traffic jam?

Begin by taking deep breaths, feeling a sense of calm and relaxation. Once this feeling of calm enters, try writing out the tasks. Then prioritize each, according to whether it is urgent or can be done another day. Remember it is humanly possible to complete only so many tasks in a day.

Be patient and understanding with yourself. After you understand that these tasks are not urgent, you will have cleared the traffic jam.

You are strong and can overcome anything. Take each day one day at a time. Your family loves you. You are a special child of God.

This is the simple method to reclaim control and relearn how to function in overwhelming situations. Even the best of human being out there, the strongest man or woman, struggles. But the fact that you struggle does not define you or make you weak.

As you overcome one difficulty, you are one step closer to achieving your ultimate goal: not being just mom, but a new and improved mom, equipped with more tools to help others—the task that you so lovingly enjoy doing.

Love,
Virmala

I was having a bad day when I first read these words. I wept, but my heart swelled with joy to read these words my daughter wrote. Realizing how much she loves me and how much she appreciates me as her mother. Such words encourage one to go forth with renewed strength and more determination. I wanted to fight, beat my depressing feelings, and become who I really am—a bright, caring, and loving person.

CHAPTER 10

Traffic Jam

When many thoughts are created in the mind and begin to confuse you, I call it "traffic jam in the mind." These thoughts enter the mind and fill it with tension and nervousness. Too many thoughts first crowd the mind and make you confused, which causes you to become upset and causes the mind to feel overworked. When this happens, you will begin to notice your energy quietly leaving you.

This is just what happens to most of you. Thoughts come frequently and queue up in your mind; next you begin to feel rushed, and it makes you feel as if there is some urgency to get it done. I emphasize that when this occurs, one should never forget that there is nothing more important than one's self and well-being. With many thoughts coming at once, this little piece of information gets forgotten. This is a common mistake we all make. You try to get on top of these many confusing thoughts and your mind become overwhelm. Small jobs become large and getting it done requires more effort. Help is required; this is your first warning that something may be wrong but always remember that you are more important.

Not every task is a high-priority task. We can learn to determine which are important and not let the total weight of the to-do list sink us into the depths of depression. These thoughts are very sneaky and can leave us confused and in a state of anxiety. Let us teach ourselves not to let thoughts push or rush us, to deal with them one at a time, and not allow them to override the intellect. You must decide the importance of the thought and if it's worth entertaining. Giving attention to a negative thought will upset you. Emotional turmoil disturbs the chemical workings of the body and causes a negative chain reaction.

How can you stop this negative chain reaction and avoid forfeiting your happiness to unruly thoughts? We can understand and apply the following tactics.

1. Remind ourselves that we can ignore or postpone some thoughts and tasks.
2. Understand that not all thoughts involve urgent matters. Some are entirely unimportant.
3. Learn to stay calm and ignore negative thoughts.
4. Treat thoughts like guests. When you are not well, you cannot entertain guests.

Neither should you entertain unproductive thoughts.

5. Love yourself, be kind to yourself, and remember you can ask for help.

This is how you can deal with this traffic jam of thoughts. You are smart and brave and can understand that a thought is only a thought. Take care of you; slow down, for there is no urgency with a thought. Remember you have the right to choose whether or not to deal with any thought.

This is what I learned from my illness, and my knowledge continues to keep me stabilized. When disturbing thoughts came, I took deep breaths and told myself that a thought could only become important if I made it important. I was truly amazed that talking to myself in this way let me take back control. Then my tension eased. This simple exercise kept me effectively in control, so please try the technique before you dismiss it. The ability to control one's mind and live without fear is the greatest freedom a human being can experience. Don't allow thoughts to send you into a panic, for your mind belong to you, and you have the right to control it.

Here is a positive exercise you should practice daily.

Speak a blessing to yourself:
God's love and grace are with me.
I must claim it.
I am happy, I am guided, and I am strong.
I am filled with kindness. I am healed.
I am deeply loved, and I am abundantly blessed.

Chapter 11

Plus Words and Minus Words

Plus words uplift, enrich, strengthen, and empower people. Plus words are positive words. The speaker of positive words and the person who hears them both receive benefits. Positive words energize the speaker and uplift the listener.

Do you ever wonder why people waste time and effort speaking negative words?

Plus words beautify our world. Many people suffer because they do not understand the power, and value of plus words. You know that words are powerful, but not everyone knows how to use their power.

You must remember that your words are powerful tools. Sometime you underestimate the impact of a thought and articulate it without considering possible effects on others. Words spoken aloud cannot be taken back, so use your words wisely and speak kindly to others. For when you speak, you and your listener are both affected.

Minus words can be destructive. They can hurt the people who hear them, and their bad energy rebounds on the speaker. Minus words bring pain and misunderstanding. Remember that you can increase your energy by speaking positively. Nothing good comes from negative words except negative energy. Minus words are filled with negative energy. Bad energy from negative speech has only negative effects on the atmosphere.

Why waste your time, effort, and energy on minus words? You neither receive nor share with hurtful words. You must understand the difference between plus words or minus words. Anger and ego fill you with negative energy and drain you of your power to be successful. Which would you take home, a bag of garbage or a bag of money? Garbage is waste. That is why it is thrown away. Minus words are like bankruptcy and bring no profit. Plus words give support and encouragement and fill all with energy.

Everybody needs positive words, as they energize us all. The effort to employ plus words is the first step in claiming your right to success.

Try to understand the value gained from listening to positive words. Stay away from bearers of negativity, for they would drain you of your energy and lead you down into a dark tunnel where you can get lost. We all pray, "God, from darkness, lead me unto light." God is positive energy; that is why we call out to Him in our times of difficulty and need. We have the power within us to make or break our fortune. It has to do with understanding, honesty, and making the effort to arrive at right decisions. Negative thoughts, however, can make you believe the worst about yourself and others. You have the right to choose the path you will walk.

Chapter 12

Support from Family and Friends

Support comes in many different forms. What is support? A kind word, a smile, a conversation, a joke, and physical assistance are all forms of support. We all need support in our lives. Look around—you will see that people are much happier when they have support. I understand what support means, how it helps, and what it can do. This is why I asked this question?

Why is it difficult for people to give support? When did we become so selfish that we now only cared for our own progress? Our world is changing rapidly. People care for themselves only. In some way or another, we are all contributing to the creation of a cold world. We must begin to pay attention. To change this world you must first understand who you are and make an effort to become better human beings. You can change the world by changing yourself. Changing other people is a task more difficult to accomplish. Sharing is our blessing, let it become the teacher.

Yesterday you were young and strong and did not plan for the future? Today you reap the benefits from your past actions. To sow good actions, share kind words, good manners, means a better future for you. Help those in need: your family, your friends, or anyone who is in need. Share a smile, share a plus word, give someone comfort, and experience that warmth that passes through your body. No riches in this world can buy this good feeling. A rich man is a man who can be happy every second of the day.

To ask for help is no easy task. We are all riddled with shame. We may feel helpless or not know how to ask. But let me share my experience with you—not asking for help means prolonging your own suffering. Don't feel that keeping silent is good; your mind fights you and tries to destroy you. I noticed that the more I stayed silent, the more I began losing my power to smile and laugh, and all I could do was cry, feel sad, and grow fearful. My negative thoughts grew stronger, and my fear grew rapidly. All this negativity crippled me into becoming someone I did not know or want to know. I did not know how to stop this destruction, but my family came to my rescue.

Along with my family, my friends and, most importantly, God came to my rescue. They all helped me, shared with me, and made me strong.

They are the ones who held me, wiped my tears, and constantly reassured me that my situation would get better. They are the ones who encouraged me to talk about what was happening and how I was feeling and to express all my concerns. Their kind words encouraged me and gave me the support I so needed. I learned from them that there is no reason to feel ashamed of any illness. We encounter many challenges; the way we choose to handle them determines there outcomes. No man is perfect, and no one is free from sickness or sorrow. Your decision to share your experience is your first step to healing. Support is a very important part of any healing process. I believe that support may be equally as important as medication.

During the trying acute phase of a depressive episode, you really learn which of your family and friends, will help you. Those who stay with you during your lowest period are the ones who care for you.

I can never repay all those loving people who helped me and comforted me. They will forever be in my heart, and my love and blessings for them will never stop. No day went by without emails, messages, cards, kind and caring words, and telephone calls. My mother, bless her, never failed to prepare meals for me with her own hands or to give me local bush medicine. My husband made breakfast each morning and made sure I took my medications. He was always ready to take me wherever I needed to go, mostly the doctor's office. My children constantly sent me messages and jokes to make me smile. My small sister never failed to send me quotes, riddles, and jokes. So many people came to my aid, and they all still continue to help me. Before my illness, I loved helping people; after it, I have an even greater desire to help others. Those who can help others are blessed.

William Prescott once said, "An obstacle is often a stepping stone." Denis Waitley said there are two primary choices in life: to accept conditions as they exist, or accept the responsibility for changing them.

I advise you to share your troubles; this is the first step to healing yourself. If you are able to help others, go ahead and do so; this might be your last chance to experience this pleasure.

Never underestimate the power of your words. Trust and have faith. God is your guide, so turn to him and seek his help.

My respect and love for my family members and friends have increased. My faith and trust in God have grown. Support begins the healing process, but you must take that first step by accepting that support. Keep in mind the rejuvenating effects of sharing. Let us all teach each other to become our brother's keeper. Good relationships are treasures to protect. Money brings greed, greed brings hate, and the negativity continues. Let us, instead, consider the resources that really are our treasures.

Chapter 13

The Return of Insecurity

The return of happiness and improved energy may make us forget to stay alert. This surge of energy is a good development, but it is not by any means an indication that we are cured. Feeling better means you are on the road to recovery. It is important to pay attention to your thoughts and make sure no negative thought slips in and shakes your small happiness. This kind of thought seems to look for an opening, a weakness, through which it can strike. It can open the way for the return of despair.

If this ever happens, remember to speak to someone. You need help. After working so hard to recover, don't let small setbacks pull you down. Fight for yourself and reclaim the right to smile. Remember that this thought is just a thought and that you are strong and beautiful, and this feeling will pass.

Your mind creates fear within you, but this fear is just a thought. This is negative energy being released. It can destroy you unless you decide to do something about it and not withdraw and hide yourself away. You have to ask yourself how you can transform this negative energy. My method was writing down all the negative thoughts. Then I would write down positive thoughts, look up inspirational quotes, and write them down. Then I reread my writing, focusing on that which was good and which would bring benefit. When you begin to see the difference in these thoughts, take a pencil and draw a line across the thoughts that drain your energy. Continue to read the positive thoughts and let positive energy be absorbed within you. This is how we get rid of negative thoughts. It is well worth the effort. Negative thoughts may stay with you longer than positive ones, so eliminating the negative ones may take time and effort. You can also replace lost energy with laughter, even though laughter may not always come easily. You have to stay focused, reminding yourself that thoughts cannot become a reality unless you act upon them. I know that I do not have to accept every thought that crosses my mind.

When joy slips away from your life, you feel empty and tired. Don't ask too many questions then, or dwell upon negative ideas. Negativity will drain you of your energy. Instead of questions, focus on self-redirection, which can help you regain your happiness and recover.

Never give up. Ask for help, Speak with people around you. Read a good book. Read inspirational quotes or watch a comedy. Don't just sit and hope for a miracle. We make the miracle happen when we stand up and take charge. Feelings come from our thoughts. It is no easy task to change these thoughts, but you have to keep trying. Write down powerful quotes in low moments, read and reread these quotes. This simple act can change the flow of your energy. Have patience, love yourself, and have faith that God is always with you. Pay attention to the thoughts that pull you down. Keep some uplifting quotes in your book and use as a rope to lift you.

There are many excuses for being down. With a positive attitude, you can only climb to higher and better ground. Music can help. Listening to music can calm an angry mind, soothe a bleeding heart, and make a sad person happy.

You must always remember that dawn comes after the darkest hour. Everything works out to enhance your life, events happen for a reason, and we have many lessons to learn. Experience makes us stronger, better, and sweeter; we all have our own unique roles to play in this world. Believe that you are special and know that you are a child of God. It is only from your experiences that you can help others. It is a privilege and blessing to help your fellow man.

Also remember to love and forgive yourself. No one is perfect. Forgiving yourself and others cures your hurt.

Chapter 14

Taking Care of You

You'll hear this question often: "Are you taking care of yourself?" You usually say, "Yes." You say "Yes" because you are eating healthy and exercising. Now I think more carefully about my answer. Yes, I am eating healthy food most of the time and doing some form of exercise, but this is taking care of the body, not the mind. How does one take care of the mind? There are many different methods to take care of the mind. From a medical aspect, the doctor might prescribe pharmacotherapy. From a holistic health standpoint, we might be advised to meditate, learn to understand your own minds, or even use some natural medication. People do not pay attention to their mental health until they are experiencing problems. We all just look at our reflection in the mirror and judge from that reflection.

This chapter's purpose is raising awareness about our need to take care of our minds. Both are extremely important body and mind.

As we grow older, our bodies go through many changes that can affect us in many different ways. We all need to learn about these changes. The aging body and mind need love, care, attention, and sometime medication. You should visit your doctor, ask questions and describe any discomfort you may be feeling. This is how you can be proactive with any health issues. Don't wait for something to go wrong. If you begin to feel strange, scared, or sad, speak to your doctor and seek medical advice. You might know someone who had experienced problems similar. Talk to that person; he or she might be able to help. Do research on anxiety and depression. Do not become disheartened; there is help, and you will get better. We learn to adjust regarding our health. We need to be proactive and pre-emptive with regard to illness. Some people quite passively allow mental illness to destroy their happiness. My friends don't give up so easily. Don't relinquish your happiness for any reason or for any person. Your happiness is your lifeline. Educate yourself, for knowledge can give you freedom. I am sharing my experiences, to help you avoid suffering and to give you hope. Sharing my knowledge is my way to give back to my fellow man. I don't want to see that lost look of despair on anyone's face. I want my readers to understand and remember to be strong and know that there is a cure.

I am sharing my experiences because depression is very challenging, and you cannot face it alone. You need family support, medical support, and strong faith. Life is enriched through knowledge, not money. A depressed person with all the money in the world but no family support, love, or care would find recovery a struggle. Medication does help, but sick people also need social support, affection, and care. Depression can happen to anyone. To be safe, we need to stay alert and pay attention to our own mental health.

There's sweetness in living in the moment, but live it wisely. Don't wait until it is too late. Taking charge of your life is your choice. Choose to make the most of every day. Quit making excuses; time waits on no one. When you take responsibility for your life and are proactive, you do not become a victim. Focus your time and energy on solutions and move forward with a smile. Remember you control the mind and it is you who must find a method to stay in control.

CHAPTER 15

Banish Shame

There is no greater satisfaction than making a positive contribution. The most beneficial means of helping you is to devote your time and energy to the difficulties of others. This distracts your mind and redirects it into a positive direction. We tend to withdraw and hold lots of secrets within ourselves when we are faced with confusion in the mind. Withholding thoughts as inner secrets create the avenue for our mind to be overpowered. This is where shame enters. It enters silently from the back door of your mind. The habit of trying to hide is what eventually brings this feeling of shame into you and prevents you from sharing or asking for help. Telling others about these difficulties and asking for help are crucial help steps. By taking this step the recovery process begins, suffering decreases, and we find our courage.

When we share our problems with others, we may help others realize how fortunate they are. Sharing is a great way to help your fellow human beings because as you explain they would understand. We all have much to give and much to learn from giving. Each good deed nourishes and increases your supply of good fortune. Do not allow your thoughts to imprison you within your own mind. That is the most dangerous thing that can happen. Sickness is no reason for you to hide away and feel embarrassed. You will recover from your illness, and life will be good again. First, stop feeling ashamed of what is happening and ask for help. You may find that others will listen and be very willing to help you. When you share, your fellow humans will acknowledge what you have said and react with kindness.

No one can help you, if you do not ask for help. People could misunderstand your silence. Some may say unkind words due to ignorance. Do not let such responses deter you from sharing your fears and problems. Talking your problems out will help you recover. Don't worry about negative responses. People who make you feel uncomfortable are very ignorant people and are now in the minority. They lack knowledge and to compensate they are hurtful or hateful.

Be brave, for bravery helps us find the cure for any sickness. The best way to change another person is to educate that person. Empty barrels make the most noise.

Enthusiasm creates joy. Joy creates more joy. The more you try, the easier it would become. Rewards always reflect what you invest.

Two ingredients are necessary for success in life—fun and fearlessness. Replace fear with faith and look for fun in everyday experiences. Remember that by speaking and expressing your feelings, you can help yourself and others to understand your situation. Help comes from understanding.

Remember that every experience holds a vital lesson. Someone said to me once, "You must stop going through your situation and start growing through it." A lesson is easier to see when we are not looking at it from a victim's perspective. Stop seeing your illness as some form of doom and try to think of it as a lesson to be mastered and an opportunity to learn. When you can think like this, you become brave, and bravery puts an end to shame. Thoughts can make or break you. Make the right choice and turn away from thoughts that could destroy you. In every challenge lies an opportunity. To run from a problem, allow that problem to become a curse, but it can be a blessing if you intend to grow through it.

Life is not a race. However, if it were a race, it would be a relay race; we would cooperate rather than compete. Begin each day with thanks, and you will see that you have more time to enjoy.

Let us start right now, be more conscious of all the good life has to offer. Do not allow your mind to be filled with fear; let faith be your support. Trust God, trust your fellow man, trust your doctor, speak out, and let us beat this mind-killing sickness. Know that you are strong, believe that God loves you, and tell yourself that you are the most fortunate soul in the world. By replacing the negative thoughts with positive ones, you would become fearless; only then will your shame vanish. When this happens, you can feel yourself breathing again. Your potential, once unleashed, is unlimited. You just have to understand this and keep faith. There is no miracle, but hard work definitely pays off.

Chapter 16

The Importance of Medication

Sickness and doctor always come in the same sentence. A doctor serves to provide medical remedies to cure ailments and disorders. Medication would help your recovery, but do not self-diagnose. In our growing world of technology, with the availability of computers, global networking, you should not have any problems finding information nor a suitable and reliable doctor. Talk to a doctor; don't just trust information you gather from the internet. Describe your symptoms and a medical doctor should be able to help you.

Facing this disorder I needed medical help and assistance. No miracle being available and my motivation to recover, I visited my doctors and listened to their advice. With trust and my strong need to recover I took my medications as prescribed. When ill, your entire mind thinks only of, I need to get better and this propelled me to research herbal remedies. I never let anyone influence me about the side effects of medication. All medication has side effects, but for recovery one has to make this choice and my choice was yes to medication. Why should I suffer? Many people have their own beliefs; do not let their belief interfere with your medication nor your doctor's treatment. Medication is a very good support for recovery but must only be taken when recommended by a doctor.

Only your doctor can prescribe your medications because he would know what your ailment required and the relevant dosages needed. No one likes to take tablets, but when it becomes necessary, we must take it. Know why you are taking certain types of medications. Remember that medication can be dangerous if taken without being prescribed by your doctor. You can listen to other people, but before you use something, ask your doctor. Prescription medication must be recommended by a doctor and it can help heal you. Most importantly, however, a good positive attitude is what you need most to recover.

Do not allow other people to influence you to stop taking your medication. Trust your doctor and yourself. Trust God. To every problem there is a solution. I believe this, and I also believe there is a reason for every situation. If we understand this, we can start curing ourselves. A positive attitude is the first step to getting better, but a mind is no easy thing to control.

My very experienced and well-qualified doctor told me, "Think of all of your tablets as a vitamin supplement for your body and not as medication." My doctor knows how to boost his patients' confidence, and his care and support helped my recover. My doctor never gave me false information or false hope. This candor is very important to a patient, for correct information helps the patient monitor his or her own progress.

I advise sufferers of depressive disorders to work toward getting well and know that soon they will be cured. Maintain focus on that goal. If we were perfect, we would be able to cure ourselves, but we are not perfect and need help from God, from our doctors, from medications, and from family and friends. Have faith and know that you will get better.

Chapter 17

How Do We Accept Help?

We all need help, but many times we cannot accept it. We all let pride, ego, and anger prevent us from learning to accept help. Some people are afraid of trying new tactics. Some are simply stubborn and don't want to accept help. Let me explain what help is all about. Someone offers help because of concern for you. Help can come from any direction or from anyone. The people, who make the effort to teach you, explain to you, correct you, or even scold you are the ones who care about you. Helping someone in any of these ways requires effort and personal time. The next time someone offers you help, please think about the time that individual is investing in you. He or she sees you as the special person. That friend or relative has chosen to help you! Think of the love, care, and respect this person has for you.

Why do you think it is hard to accept help? Some people may fear change; they may fear what will happen if they try new tactics. We need to understand why we are reluctant to accept help.

Habitual modes of thought and ego may prevent us from accepting help. These may block any good change in your life. This is why you must understand your reasons for not accepting help.

Our habits of stubbornness can prevent us from having a better life. Not all thoughts bring benefit. Bear in mind that sometimes it is difficult to stop or control these thoughts that come so fast and furiously into your head. Thoughts created with negativity can create lots of pain and unhappiness for you, first and foremost, but they can also create a chain reaction and destroy the care and love coming to you from family members and friends. If you do not pay heed to these thoughts and let them become powerful, it is very hard to rise above them. A person must be alert for negative habits of thought that bring unhappiness. Share these thoughts and feeling. These baseless fears are not normal; you must never feel that you have to accept them and be silent about them. The more you talk about your fearful thoughts, the less power they will have. When you express and expose such thoughts, you take back power and gain control over yourself. Control your own mind and emotions by exposing these thoughts, no matter how silly and trivial they may seem to you. Only by talking will this fear decrease; then confidence will replace it. You will become less angry and more willing to accept help. Remember that it takes time for someone to make you happy. If you were not special—if they did not love, care for, and respect you—they would never sacrifice their time. Money cannot pay for caring person's time. Understanding the value of others' time and energy is a very important aspect of self-improvement, happiness, and progress. Your goal is to become happy and free of unfounded fears. A person in a pathological mental state, an abnormal state, is fearful, filled with panic, afraid to make changes and unwilling to accept help, will and can gradually be destroyed and hurt. There are many tools available to make these thoughts and problems go away FOREVER. It's like when you learned to walk for the first time; you fell down many times, you cried, but your parents never allowed you to give up. When you had mastered the art of walking, priceless joy followed. Your success allowed you to believe in yourself and your abilities. It let you think, "I can do this all by myself!"

Similarly, with the thoughts that are created in your mind; you have to make an effort, talk about it, share your feelings with your many loved ones, and create your support network. Be brave and accept their help and learn, for only then you will gradually begin realizing what a powerful human being you are. You must allow yourself to take the first step, saying, "I need help, and I will accept this help." If a habit or tactic is not working for you, why are you holding onto it? Get rid of it and use another method. It is only by trying that you will be successful in controlling your own mind.

People actually become failures when they fail to try. Sincere effort brings success.

Do not let preconceptions and habits prevent you from trying, listening, and accepting help. Let me tell you a secret. Your thoughts that are created in your own mind can sometimes be your worst enemies. Do not trust them.

Change is good. Think of change as a new outfit—how fast would you give up an old one for a new one? See the smile on your face and experience the joy this new outfit brings. Accepting help to change, you will feel joy, great relief, and a new sense of personal peace. Confidence will rebound, and you will be able to smile and speak freely again.

Our habitual pathological habits of thought can silence us, make us withdraw, make us loose our confidence, and replace it with fear. The fears of never being able to speak freely again make a person feel enclosed in a cage with his or her own insecurities. Such thoughts may indeed be your own thoughts, but they are not your friends. Negative thoughts drain your energy. Don't think you can set aside these thoughts all by yourself, but know that with help and your cooperation you can destroy them and prevent them from coming into your mind. Thoughts become a habit, and you can always change a bad habit into a good one.

Learn to accept the help that you have around you. When someone offers help, listen with an open mind, and then it would become easy. Don't feel help is aimed at putting you down. The person offering help is not trying to put you down or make you look stupid. Help is exactly what its definition states: assistance. It is intended to enable you to become better and aimed at making you happier.

When you refuse help, you prolong your suffering, and you also make those who love you suffer. Help is great! It's the first step to healing yourself from the inside. We all need help, and accepting help is not a sign of weakness. Anger is the cause for your hurt, and yet you will continue to allow this action to become your guide to pull you down. With help, a person can build courage. Your thoughts prevent you from accepting help because they do not want you to become strong and free. The fears they create lack any realistic substance. When we do not expose these inner thoughts, which are continually abusing us emotionally, we continue to feel the effects of them. Remember you have courage, but thoughts infiltrate your mind and put fear there. Be alert and careful; these thoughts may be ours, but they can abuse us to such an extent that we totally forget who we are and how powerful we really can be.

To be alert means be aware of your thoughts. Sift it and weed out the negatives, or tell someone whom you can trust. If no one is around, write them down. By doing this, you are exposing it and releasing it from your mind, and then you become free from the crowd of negative thoughts.

As a warning, do not feel that everyone can be trusted. Be careful whom you choose to trust. Just like your thoughts, there are both good and bad people around us. The bad people are the ones who prey on vulnerable people like you. Don't let the wrong person into your life on the pretense that they want to help, for they have their own agendas. They want to weaken you and take advantage. So my advice is to find a trustworthy person. When you need help, be sure to seek help.

Chapter **18**

Believe in Yourself

Believe that you are beautiful, cherish your uniqueness, and be who you are. Trust yourself to overcome your challenges. Be strong when you can and cry when you can't. Embrace the present. Never be afraid to love yourself. You are your strength. Anyone can fall at some point. You must believe in yourself, understand who you really are and have faith that you can overcome. Today your mind may pull you in a tumultuous direction, but it doesn't mean that you are not peaceful, just because your thoughts filled you with negativity today. Both positive and negative exist and therefore if a positive can become a negative vice versa it can be also.

During the lower phases of my illness, my sister Lisa repeatedly told me never to give up on myself. She kept reminding me that I was a very strong person with many good qualities. Without such support, I would still be struggling today. "Thank you" cannot express the extent of my gratitude to all who helped me. I may have only mentioned one name, but many have offered great help in my healing process. My husband, children, sisters, brother, parents, and friends have all supported me, giving me the strength to keep believing in myself. Words are not adequate to express my gratitude and appreciation to all these beautiful people. To express my gratitude, I can proudly say that I am well. Today I am happy, and it's all because I believed in myself. I am also happy due to those who held my hand and guided me through these difficult times. They encouraged me to believe and to hold onto my faith, and this is what helped to heal me.

When you become sick, everything around you seems bleak and dull. At this time you need to draw from your inner strength, and your faith should grow stronger. We are strong souls filled with all good virtues, but the negativity around us and the overflow of negative thoughts weaken us.

To stay powerful, keep powerful thoughts in mind.

- Choose to hear the good in what others say to you.
- Think of the good people around you.
- Be happy with yourself.
- Hold onto God's hand. He is always waiting for you to call on Him.
- Remember that you are the best *you* there ever will be.

Positive thoughts may keep negative thoughts at bay, but we need other help as well. We need to take all prescribed medication, get proper rest, play music, and let ourselves become absorbed in conversations. Being alone is not helpful; negative thoughts may come readily to an idle mind.

Watching comedies can help the mind. Laughter can help restore self-confidence and sweet serenity. With the return of your confidence, you will automatically begin to regain your faith in yourself, averting low self-esteem.

Not everyone is sensitive to other people's problems. Instead of listening to an insensitive person, read a book with a positive message. Transform negative energy with a positive quote. This can help restore your faith in yourself and raise your energy level.

You are a powerful person with abundant of good qualities and positive energy. You radiate light. Remain mindful that thoughts are very strong. Keep alert; keep positive thoughts in your mind and remember that only you can give these thoughts power. Read a powerful verse; write it or say it aloud. This technique can dissolve problematic thoughts. Let your light outshine these waste thoughts and burn them away.

Your inner light never diminishes, though it may seem to dim. Your light is unlimited; it shines more brightly than the sun. Feel that strength within and remain powerful. You are born powerful and will always be a winner. Smile and keep reminding yourself that you are an energy source with no power outage.

CHAPTER 19

Managing Anger

Anger may flare within an unsettled mind. Anger can be a very strong emotion that locks us away in a jail of sorrow. No one likes to stay upset and angry because it is painful. People can become so angry that they stop speaking, becoming even violent. Anger brings sorrow, and it's hard to understand the damaging impact while it is happening. Hate, fury, and sorrow crowd out goodness. We see but do not see. We hear but do not hear. The mind is debilitated by anger. You may not know this but anger depletes your energy and causes sorrow. Anger is a very hard emotion to eliminate. One can stay angry for days, weeks, months, or years. Such is the negativity that anger brings. How do we stop anger from taking control? We need power; we need the energy to fight anger. Anger is like any other negative emotion that grips us and robs us of our smiles and happiness. To control anger, we have to stay alert and attempt to understand what triggers it. Most importantly, we must think of our own health. Did you know that these negative emotions steal from us?

Why are we allowing this to happen? We must seek what is good for us. Anger can't be reverse by telling ourselves that we aren't angry. As with academic study a lot of hard work is necessary to succeed, in the same way managing anger takes effort. This effort provides you with a healthier life and higher energies level. When angry, first pay attention to the reason for your anger. Second, ask yourself if anger was necessary. These are the easy parts. You are your best caregiver and must do what is best and right for yourself. Remember that you love yourself. Most of the time anger is directed to your love ones. If you remember your love for that person at your time of anger symptom, it may help calm your mind. Ask yourself; is it necessary to lose my peace of mind over some trivial situation? People are going to have different opinions. But you can agree to disagree. It is not your best decision to give up a positive mind-set over differing opinions. This choice is yours; don't let thoughts pull you in the wrong direction. Anger takes us down the road of sorrow and unhappiness.

We must keep our uniqueness in mind, for we are really gentle, sweet and charming. How do we keep this positive energy? We make God our Guide and remember to love ourselves.

The people suffering from a chemical imbalance, these emotions are much harder to manage. They struggle with all emotions, good and bad, but have to work twice harder to keep calm and accept help. This emotion can eat at you until it destroys you. Anger can lead them onto the road of sorrow, depletes their energy and with no will to live. Never accept things that will injure you. Realize how fortunate you are to be in control because when you lose your managing power your fight is more difficult.

Eliminating anger is no easy task. I recommend allowing your loved ones to help. Keep a good book at hand to read. Read a passage that will calm you. Turn to God and speak to Him. God always listen. He will send an angel to lend you support. Those who choose to eliminate anger opt to live, be happy, be filled with energy, and respect themselves. Make a habit of dealing with one thought at a time. Learn to listen to your loved ones and to trust God. Have faith in yourself. Giving your thoughts the power to control may prove disastrous and make you unhappy. Be vigilant to avoid this sadness and depletion. Never say that it is impossible. The only people who fail are those who have not tried.

Chapter 20

Essential Self-Management: A Short List

1. Remember that God is with you and you can speak to Him anytime and anywhere.
2. Exercise replenishes lost energy.
3. Trust your loved ones; they can support you. Remember it is no crime to accept help.
4. You must take care of yourself; pay attention to what is happening within you. Never allow your thoughts to pull you down. Continue working on yourself to stay strong.
5. Always read material that can uplift you. Listen to music.

These are some keys to strength and empowerment to an enjoyable life. Sharing your time, your knowledge, or abilities to help others will make you stronger, happier, and more energetic. Stay on top of the game, and never forget to be alert. Nurture hope. Hope is our cure, and faith is our strength.

Nourish this positive energy. When you shine, your light will brighten someone else's life. Do you know how important your smile is that it enhances others' lives? Never forget that you have that power to uplift others and generate your own strength so that you can look forward to the future.

In a world where a vast amount of information is readily available, we should be cautions on how and what we accept. Only when we understand this knowledge can we apply and enjoy the results. Find and use available material. Information equals more knowledge. Knowledge is the key to success.

As a special person whom God has blessed with life, you must make the best of what you have, which means listening, learning, teaching others, and trying to make the best possible choices.

Sometimes we talk ourselves out of doing something healing for ourselves. We're too busy or too tired. But that is when we most need to take time to care for ourselves. Always listen to your heart. What does it want? Listen to your body. What does it need? Trust what you hear. Difficulties come into our life, but it brings a lesson. Learn, grow, smile and share. This too will pass and you will once again be you.

JUST FOR YOU

A tardy bit tired,
A small shiver inside.
It moves quietly.
With such stillness,
that one cannot detect its movement.

I feel restless
I feel scared
I feel nervous
I feel weird.

What is this thing?
This feeling that is so strong.
Where did it come from?
Where would it go?
And what would it do?

I need to know,
I want to know,
I stood quietly
Feeling and seeing
Thinking and wishing
Knowing, yet not wanting to know.

This alarming feeling
wanting to take me
Down that dark lengthy road,

But I am already tired.
What is the solution?
Where to find that key,
To release this feeling
To set it free from me.

Is it that thing call fear?
Or is the feeling of being lost.

I look up
I let the smile flow out
Just as busy as an hurricane
Pushing out that old feeling
That tired feeling
Oh I know, I know!
I am capable
I am strong
I can see the end
It is so near.
My heart lifts,
my brain race
I would be prepared
Before that day reaches.

Nothing is too much.
Nothing is too difficult
The only thing to create a block,
I have in my control.
My smile is my energy
My brain feels all happy
I know I can do this
I know I would succeed

There is no need for me to worry
No need to fret
For I am an Angel
Always racing fast ahead.

ABOUT THE AUTHOR

Who is Leela Maharaj? Leela Maharaj is a citizen of Trinidad and Tobago. She is a simple person who enjoys helping others and sharing with them. For this reason, she decided to share her experiences. Leela Maharaj is married and has a family.

When she began to suffer from depression, she experienced an abrupt transition from her accustomed strength and happiness to a weak, fearful state. She found herself in an unknown tunnel, totally lost. Leela decided to share her experience in the hope of helping others. This silent monster, as she calls it, comes suddenly and steals a person's identity, rendering that person more lost than Little Bo Peep's sheep. Her slogan became "I am strong, and I will overcome."

This book is about her experience with anxiety and depression.

Printed in the United States
By Bookmasters